GW00729082

BRANCH LINES TO TUNBRIDGE WELLS

Vic Mitchell and Keith Smith

Design – Deborah Goodridge

ISBN 0906520 32 0

First published July 1986

© Middleton Press, 1986.

Published by Middleton Press
              Easebourne Lane
              Midhurst, West Sussex.
              GU29 9AZ
              ☎ 073 081 3169

Typeset by CitySet · Bosham 573270

Printed & bound by Biddles Ltd,
              Guildford and Kings Lynn.

CONTENTS

INDEX

GEOGRAPHICAL SETTING

The lines contained in this album are entirely within the Weald, Oxted being at the foot of the North Downs and Lewes and Polegate being similarly related to the South Downs. All three lines cross three or four miles of Wealden Clay before rising onto the central sandstone mass of the Weald, formed by the Hastings Beds.

The Oxted line passes over several tributaries of the River Medway whilst the Lewes line crosses the watershed near Crowborough to follow the River Ouse southwards. The Cuckoo Line from Polegate is in the valley of the Cuckmere River north of Hailsham and then crosses the River Rother south of Mayfield.

All maps contained in this album are to the scale of 25″ to 1 mile, unless otherwise stated.

ACKNOWLEDGEMENTS

Our grateful thanks go to all the photographers mentioned in the credits, many of whom have supplied much additional information. We also wish to thank Mrs E. Fisk, N. Stanyon and our wives for assistance with the text and N. Langridge for providing many of the tickets.

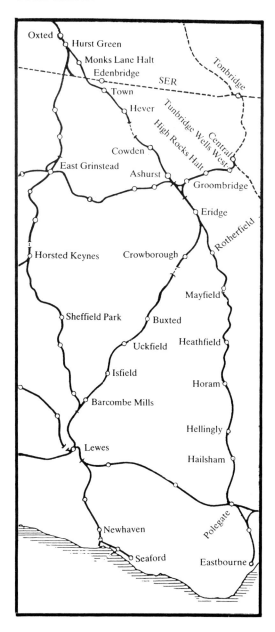

(East Grinstead – Tunbridge Wells West appears in *Branch Lines to East Grinstead*)

HISTORICAL BACKGROUND

The London Brighton and South Coast Railway Company's line reached Lewes and Polegate in the mid-1840's, and the South Eastern Railway's route to Tunbridge Wells came into operation in 1845.

Branches from Polegate to Hailsham and Eastbourne were opened on 14th May 1849.

The next branch in the district was from Lewes to Uckfield and came into use on 11th October 1858, public services commencing on 18th October.

In the north of the area, the LBSCR branch from Three Bridges to East Grinstead was extended to an independent station at Tunbridge Wells on 1st October 1866. The line was linked to Uckfield with a single track from Groombridge on 3rd August 1868.

Single track was provided by the LBSCR in 1872 between the two Tunbridge Wells stations, but it was not used until 1st February 1876 and then only by SER trains.

A further single line was opened from Hailsham to Heathfield on 5th April 1880 and extended north to Groombridge on 1st September of that year.

The route from Oxted to East Grinstead came into use on 10th March 1884 and the direct line to Tunbridge Wells via Edenbridge first saw passenger traffic on 1st October 1888.

The final development in the district was the doubling of the Uckfield line in 1894, with the elimination of parallel single tracks south of Eridge by the formation of Redgate Mill Junction.

* * * * *

The first line in the district to be closed was the Cuckoo Line north of Hailsham. This took place on 13th June 1965, the section between Polegate and Hailsham remaining open until 8th September 1968.

The link between Uckfield and Lewes ceased on 23rd February 1969, but Groombridge and Tunbridge Wells West stations did not lose their passenger trains until 6th July 1985, when the Eridge-Tonbridge service was withdrawn.

PASSENGER SERVICES

All services were operated by the LBSCR and initially were centred upon Tunbridge Wells – hence the title of this album. One exception was a SER service between Eastbourne and Charing Cross via Eridge and Tonbridge, in 1884–85. All trains on the Uckfield and Hailsham lines were directed at this important town instead of London, until about 1914 when a triangular junction was formed west of Groombridge. The introduction of direct London services reduced the importance of Groombridge as a junction station, also the number of through trains between Tunbridge Wells and London. To compensate for this loss, slip coaches were shed from some down trains whilst passing through Ashurst. Eridge increased in importance, becoming the point where London trains were divided for the two lines south. Also at this time, more of the London – Tunbridge Wells trains were diverted to run via East Grinstead, instead of the direct line to Oxted.

The advent of World War I delayed the full introduction of these improvements and at one period caused the temporary withdrawal of passenger services, except in the business hours. This was due to the movement of troops and materials to large hutted camps in the Forest Row and Crowborough areas.

The formation of the Southern Railway in 1923 resulted in some reduction in journey times and the elimination of slip coaches. Sleepy little Ashurst then became a junction station for many years and some services were extended to Tonbridge.

Reduction of scheduled trains was necessary during World War II but many extras were run, such as special non-stop workmen's trains between London, Crowborough and Mayfield.

British Railways inherited this complicated and inconsistent pattern of services and in 1956 introduced a regular interval hourly timetable on the lines, with additional trains in the rush hours. Diesel-electric units began to appear in 1962, running to the steam schedules and from 1971 Groombridge and Tunbridge Wells West were only served by the hourly Eridge – Tonbridge shuttle, until it was withdrawn on 6th July 1985.

1890

(Upper timetable — Brighton, Lewes, Uckfield, Groombridge and Tunbridge Wells)

Fares.	Central Station.	Week Days.	Sndys		Week Days.	Sundays.
1 cl. 2 cl. 3 cl.		mrn mrn mrn aft aft aft aft aft aft		Tunbridge Junc..dep	mrn mrn aft aft aft	
s.d. s.d. s.d.	Brighton ....dep	7 10 8 10 9 32 1155 1 40 4 30 5 40 5 40 7 15 9 0 2 58 8	Tunbridge Wells(S.E)	7 45 1042 1 15 4 5	6 30
0 8 0 6 0 4	„ (Londn Rd.) „	7 13 8 13 9 35 1158 1 43 4 33 5 43 5 43 7 18 9 3 2 88 8 11	„ L.B. & S.C.	7 55 1052 1 25 4 15	6 40
0 9 0 7 0 4½	Falmer „			Groombridge	7 25 8 26 1013 1112 2 4 46	7 15 9 5 4
1 6 1 0 0 8	Lewes „	7 32 8 32 9 55 1218 2 5 4 53 6 2 6 21 7 38 9 32 9 52 8 50	Eridge	7 30 8 30 1039 1117 2 8 4 51	7 21 5 15
2 2 1 6 0 11½	Barcombe Mills	7 40 8 40 10 3 1226 2 14 3 1 „ 6 30 7 47 9 40 10 1 8 59	Crowborough	7 43 8 52 1039 1135 2 26 5 10	7 29 5 25
2 9 2 0 1 1¼	Isfield „	7 46 8 46 1232 2 20 5 7 „ 6 36 7 53 9 46 10 7 9 5	Buxted	7 48 8 52 1039 1135 2 26 5 10	7 35 5 34
3 4 2 4 1 4½	Uckfield „	7 54 8 56 1013 1241 2 32 5 14 6 17 6 43 7 59 10 1 1013 9 17	Uckfield	7 50 9 0 1045 1144 2 34 5 16 5 40 7 0 7 55 9 30	7 46 5 43
3 9 2 8 1 7	Buxted „	7 59 9 1 1018 1246 2 37 „ 6 22 „ 10 1 1024 9 27	Isfield	7 56 9 6 b 1150 2 40 5 22 5 46 7 5 8 1 9 36	7 52 5 50
4 8 3 3 1 11½	Crowborough	8 10 9 12 1029 1258 2 49 „ 6 31 „ 1026 1045 9 43	Barcombe Mills	8 2 9 12 „ 1156 2 46 5 28 5 52 7 11 8 7 9 42	7 58 5 57
5 8 3 3 2 3	Eridge 77	8 18 9 20 1038 1 7 2 58 „ 6 47 „ 1026 1045 9 47	Lewes 72 ..arr	8 11 9 21 12 12 6 2 5 6 36 6 37 7 20 8 15 9 50	8 6 6 5
5 9 4 0 2 5	Groombridge	8 24 9 26 1044 1 15 3 4 „ 6 47 „ 1032 1051 9 50	Falmer „	9 32 „ 1220 3 7 5 50 6 25 7 30 8 28	8 14 6 12
6 0 4 3 2 6	Tunbridge Wells	8 32 9 34 1052 1 21 3 12 „ 6 55 „ 1040 1059 9 57	Brighton(Lon.Rd.) „	8 27 9 40 1119 1229 3 16 5 59 6 34 7 38 8 47 10 6 4 39 6 24	8 14 6 12
	6th. East.. „	10 5 1 35 3 24 7 19	(Central) „	8 32 9 46 1125 1235 3 23 6 6 6 40 7 44 8 55 1015 4 47 6 37	8 19 6 27
	Tunbridge Jn..ar	1015 1 46 3 35 7 30			

☞ For other Trains between Tunbridge Wells and Eridge, see page 77. a Stops to set down 1 & 2 class Passengers.

b Stops by signal to take up 1 & 2 class Passengers.

TUNBRIDGE WELLS WEST, HAILSHAM, and EASTBOURNE.—Southern.

Down. — Week Days.

Miles	Station														
	Tunbridge Wells West dp	mrn	6 57 7 28	9 7 1040 12 8	1 50		4 50 5 55								
	Groombridge ... arr		7 3 7 33	9 13 1046 1211	1 55		4 31 5 55								
218	VICTORIA ...dep	Arrive Mayfield at 7 51 mrn	5 30	8 37	11X18	1155		4 25 5 60							
218	LONDON BRIDGE „		5 18		h		2810 4 44								
	Groombridge ...dep		7 34	9 14 1047 1219	1 58		4 32 5 56								
5	Eridge		7 12 7 39	9 20 1054 1218 12 23	2 15		4Y48 6 H 9								
8½	Rotherfield & Mark Cross		7 21 7 50	9 28 11 5 12 31	2 15		4 56 6 17								
11	Mayfield		7 36 8 1	9 37 1117 12 40	2 24		5 6 6 26								
14	Heathfield		7 49 8 13	9 50 1130 12 53	2 39		5 22 6 38								
17½	Waldron & Horeham Road		7 58	9 1140 1 2	2 48		5 32 6 47								
20¾	Hellingly		8 9	9 1149 1 11	2 56		5 41 6 56								
22½	Hailsham	7 0	8 13 9 55	1027 1130 1155 1 18	1 47 2 23	4 35 5 23	5 47 7 1								
25½	Polegate 195, 204	arr 7 7	8 19	10 29 1137 12 4	1 26 1 54 3 10 4 44	4 42 5 30	5 55 7 9								
		dep 7 14	8 33	1010 10 31	12 5 1 56 3 13 4 51	5 15 5 32	5 58 7 10								
27½	Hampden Park †		8 38	1010 10 37	2 2 3 18 3 50	5 14 5 37	6 27 16								
29	Eastbourne ... arr	7 24	8 45	1015 12 42 1218	1 36 2 9 3 27 4 59	5 19 5 42	6 77 21								

Down. — Week Days—Continued. | Sundays.

Station	aft	aft aft aft			mrn mrn	mrn mrn	aft aft aft aft aft
Tunbridge Wells West dp	6 45	6 53 8 9			1020	4 12	8 23
Groombridge	6 51	6 59 8 15			1026	4 18	8 31
218 VICTORIA ...dep	5 5	6X6			8 50	2 30	7 5
218 LONDON BRIDGE	5 21	8 10			8 30		6 46
Groombridge ...dep	6 52	7 4			1027	4 19	8 32
Eridge	6 58	7 9 8 17			1033	4 24	8 38
Rotherfield & Mark Cross	7 6	7 26	9J17	Weds. Sats.	1041	4 33	8 45
Mayfield	7 15	7 35	9 25		1050	4 43	5 56
Heathfield		7 47 8 10	9 46 1015		11 5	4 577 28	9 12
Waldron & Horeham Road	7 37	8 2	9 58 1023		1114	5 97 37	9 19
Hellingly	7 47	8 32	10 8 1032		1123	5 197 47	9 28
Hailsham	7 52	8 4 8 44 9	1013 1037		1131	2 25 5 26 7 53 8 48	9 37
Polegate 195, 204	arr 8 1	8 52 9 57	1022 1045		7 23 9 18 1013 1139	2 32 5 33 48 4 8 55	9 45 10 9 58
	dep 8 6	8 53 9 57	1022 1046		7 41 9 15 1015 1141	2 35 5 36 4 48 5 59 42 10 0	
Hampden Park †	8 11	8 59	1026 1051		7 49 9 23 1019 1146	2 40 5 42 8 49 9 46 10 4	
Eastbourne ... arr	8 16	9 3 10 3 1031 1056			7 52 9 26 1024 1151	2 45 5 47 8 1 59 9 51 10 9	

Up. — Week Days.

Miles	Station	mrn mrn mrn mrn	mrn mrn	mrn mrn mrn mrn	aft aft	aft aft
	Eastbourne ...dep	6 35 7 53 8 40 9 48 11 0	1215 1235 2 48 3 35 4	4 4 34 4 25 5 50 6 36		
2	Hampden Park †	arr 6 41 7 58 „ 9 53 11 8	1219 1259 2 52 3 39 „	4 8 38 4 30 5 55 6 42		
4½	Polegate	arr 6 49 8 48 49 8 58 11 16	1225 5 2 57 3 44 4 11	4 13 4 43 5 26 1 6 49		
		dep 6 50 8 58 54 10 3 11 17	1230 1 73 13 3 4 64 11	4 43 4 485 10 16 6 49		
7½	Hailsham	7 0 8 16 9 2 10 16 1125	1238 1 213 213 3 54 19	4 58 5 15 36 17 12 6 53		
9½	Hellingly	7 8 8 22 10 22	1 24 3 59 4X29	4 59 6 13 7 8		
12½	Waldron & Horeham Road	7 12 8 26 10 31	1 45 4 19	5 30 6 40 7 12		
15	Heathfield	7 21 8 44 10 43	1 57 4 31	5 42 6 52 7 26		
18½	Mayfield	7 40 8 36 8 57 10 55	2 5 4 38	6 7 8		
21½	Rotherfield & Mark Cross	7 50 8 44 9 11 4	2 5 4 38	6 13 7 14		
24	Eridge 220, 224	arr 7 59 8 14 8 54 9 40 11 14	2 26 4 56	6 23 7 20		
26½	Groombridge 220 ...arr	8 19 5 59 9 30 11 20	2 26 4 56	6 23 7 20		
6½	220 LONDON BRIDGE ...arr	9 30 10 810 42 „	9 30 11 20			
6½	220 VICTORIA „	9 42 1014 10X30	1X36 3X41	6 29		
	Groombridge ...dep	8 18 8 59 9 31 11 20	1 24 4 57	6 21 7 25		
29½	Tunbdg Wells W. 270 arr	8 27 9 4 9 38 11 29	2 34	6 31 7 35		

Up. — Wk. Dys.—Contd. | Sundays.

Station	aft aft aft	mrn mrn mrn mrn aft aft aft aft aft
Eastbourne ...dep	7 30 9 1010 1023	7 88 5 9 3410 242 0 5 40 6 15 8 30 9 30 1028
Hampden Park †	7 34 9 1410 35	7 13 8 9 38 1042 5 5 45 6 15 8 24 8 341026
Polegate	arr 7 41 9 2010 45	7 19 8 15 9 43 1023 2 11 5 50 6 21 8 29 8 39 1031
	dep 7 41 9 3410 45	7 21 8 16 8 52 1034 1038 196 05 6 30 8 41 1035
Hailsham	7 54 9 4210 53	7 28 8 23 10 0 1052 9 6 06 30 8 379 491043
Hellingly	47 59 9J47	7 38 8 26 „ 1043 „ 6 35
Waldron & Horeham Road	47 59 8J58	7 48 8 37 „ 1052 „ 6 18 6 44
Heathfield	7 56	7 56 „ 11 5 „ 6 28 6 54
Mayfield	8 7 8 23	8 17 „ 1119 „ 7 4
Rotherfield & Mark Cross	8 16	8 17 „ 1126 „ 7 20
Eridge 220, 224	8 25	8 26 „ 1137 „ 7 29
Groombridge 220 ...arr	8 29	8 32 „ 1145 „ 7 35
220 LONDON BRIDGE ...arr	1016	1018 „ 9 17
220 VICTORIA „	1010	1020 „ 1 41
Groombridge ...dep	8 30	8 33 „ 1148 „ 7 34
Tunbdg Wells W. 270 dp	8 37	9 2 „ 1 43 „ 7 43

☞ For other Trains

BETWEEN PAGE
London, Polegate, and Eastbourne ...198
Tunbridge Wells West and Groombridge ...220
Tunbridge Wells West and Eridge ...224

A Passengers with hand luggage may change at East Croydon into the 6 8 aft. from Victoria.
b Arrives at 9 14 mrn.
c Arrives at 10 14 mrn.
d Except Saturdays.
h Arrives at 2 13 aft.
H Arrives at 5 2 aft.
D On Saturdays leaves Cannon Street at 12 16 and calls at London Bridge (S. E. & C.) High Level at 12 20 aft.
J Arrives at 9 11 aft.
K On Saturdays, also on alternate Wednesdays (Asylum visiting days only).
R Leaves at 2 30 aft. on Saturdays.
W Wednesdays and Saturdays.
X Through Trains to and from Heathfield Line Stations.
Y Arrives 4 38 aft.
† Station for Willingdon.

1924

1. Oxted – Ashurst
OXTED

1. An agreement between the LBSCR and the SER gave the latter rights to the area north of its Redhill – Tonbridge line. When the Croydon, Oxted and East Grinstead Railway was completed in 1884 joint ownership was necessary as it was to be operated by the LBSCR. (Lens of Sutton)

SOUTHERN RAILWAY.
Issued subject to the Bye-laws, Regulations & Conditions in the Company's Bills and Notices.

OXTED

Excess Fare 7D.

Not valid without production of Return Half of Original Ticket

0581   0581

2. Another southward view, taken many years later, indicates an increase in milk traffic and shows the sleepers exposed to view. The earlier practice could conceal unsound timber. A trio of early horse boxes are also to be seen. (Lens of Sutton)

3. A northbound train approaches the station in May 1952 and passes over the A25, the country lane on the extreme left of the picture and on the right of the map. It was this deep valley that limited the length of the goods yard head shunt. (D.B. Clayton)

4. No. 34101 *Hartland* stands at the head of the 6.10 pm departure from Victoria on 19th July 1961. This train divided here; the front part running via Eridge to Brighton (arr. 8.11) and the rear portion leaving, ten minutes after arrival, for all stations to Tunbridge Wells West via East Grinstead. (R.S. Greenwood)

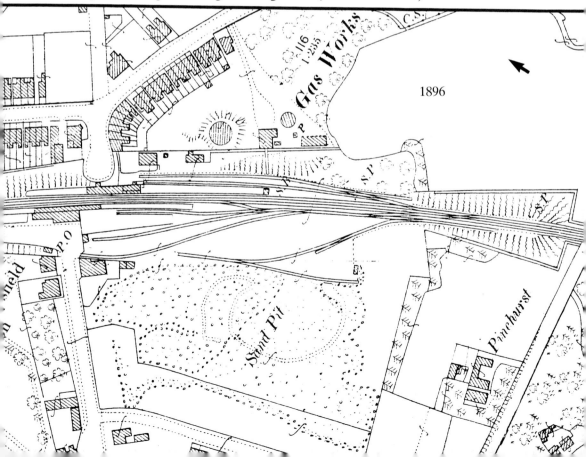

5. Twenty minutes earlier, H class no. 31005 waits to leave with the 6.28 all stations to Tunbridge Wells West via Edenbridge, having connected with the 5.37 from London Bridge. In 1986, the bay was being re-sleepered, as it will presumably be used by diesel trains to Uckfield when London – East Grinstead services are electrified in 1987. (R.S. Greenwood)

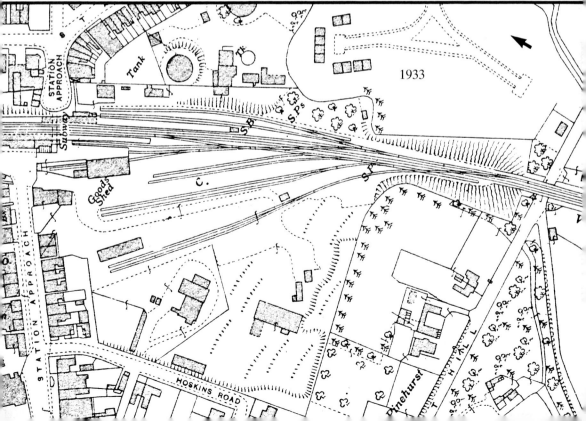

HURST GREEN

HURST GREEN MOTOR HALT, OXTED.

1933

Hurst Green Halt

Hurst Green Junction

S.R.

CROYDON, OXTED & EAST GRINSTEAD RAILWAY

6. The halt was opened on 1st June 1907 and for many years only motor trains stopped there. This one is being propelled on the down line by a Terrier 0–6–0 T and driven from the leading end of the coach, one of the distinctive "Balloon" trailers.
(Lens of Sutton)

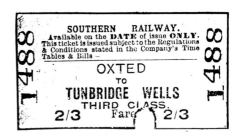

SOUTHERN RAILWAY.
Available on the DATE of issue ONLY.
This ticket is issued subject to the Regulations & Conditions stated in the Company's Time Tables & Bills –

OXTED
TO
TUNBRIDGE WELLS
THIRD CLASS.
2/3   Fare   2/3

L 1488   1488

7. A southward view from the road bridge in June 1923 shows the 1884 line to East Grinstead continuing into the distance; the 1888 route to Edenbridge branching to the left and an ample provision for waiting bottoms, better than many *stations* today.
(Late E. Wallis)

8. By 29th April 1960, work was progressing on the up platform of a new station. This would accommodate 12 coaches instead of the two that could just fit at the platform in the distance. (R. Randell Collection)

9. The station was opened on 12th June 1961 and was no longer a "Halt". It was fitted with traditional SR pattern hexagonal lampshades and is photographed here in 1963 with no. 31005, seen earlier at Oxted. (S.C. Nash)

MONKS LANE HALT

10. This was another halt that came into use in 1907 (1st July) but, unlike Hurst Green, no residential development took place and it closed on 11th September 1939. This is the up platform and only the concrete supports of the waiting shelters could be seen in 1986. (Lens of Sutton)

Other views of Oxted and Hurst Green are to be found in *Branch Lines to East Grinstead*.

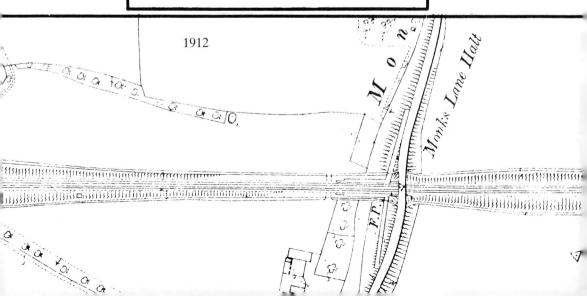

EDENBRIDGE TOWN

12. The suffix "Town" was added on 1st May 1896, which helps to date these photographs. As there has recently been a few examples of joint ventures between BR and local organisations to undertake station restoration, one hopes that this will occur here. It must be a progressive town to have recently combined its churches of different denominations. (M.G. Joly Collection)

11. About 1¼ miles before reaching this station, we pass under the former SER main line in the 319 yd. long Edenbridge tunnel. In 1986, the fine south-west facade remained little altered, as it approached its centenary. (M.G. Joly Collection)

13. With the former cattle dock siding on the left, class 4P 2–6–4T no. 42101 heads south past the signal box on the 11.8 am Victoria – Eastbourne/Brighton service on 2nd April 1952. (R.C. Riley)

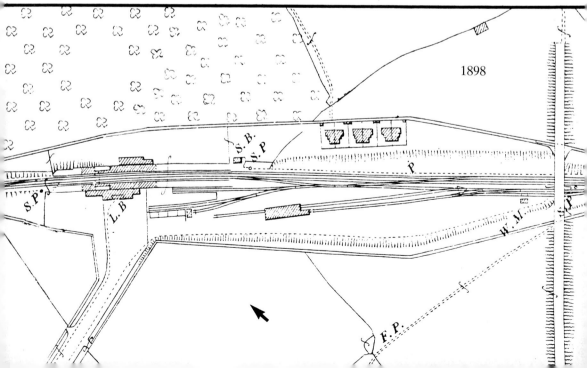

1898

14. In 1954 the goods yard was still busy and fairly tidy. It closed on 10th July 1968 but the coal staithes remain in use. (D. Cullum)

15. Many of the railway's past uses have been forgotten. This is a lengthy pigeon special from Newcastle, bound for Crowborough where the birds would be released. The locomotives are class U1 no. 31899 and West Country class no. 34019 *Bideford*. The cottages also belonged to the railway. (S.C. Nash)

HEVER

16. Looking towards Oxted soon after the line opened, we can admire the polychromatic brickwork employed here and at the other stations on the route. The signal box was opposite the entrance to the goods yard and survived until the advent of the SR. (M.G. Joly Collection)

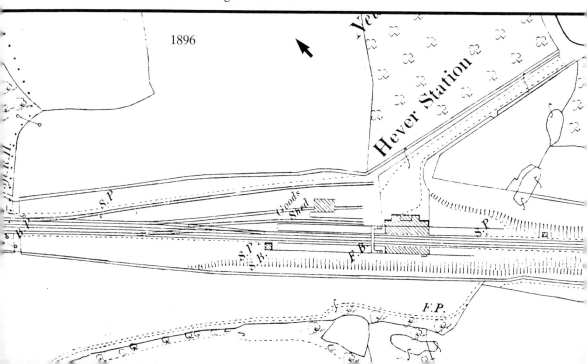

17. In 1954 grass was growing on much of the platform area as the 13th-century moated Hever Castle was attracting fewer visitors by rail than in earlier years – it is over a mile walk from the station. The goods yard closed in the following year. (R.C. Riley)

18. H class no. 31543 departs for Oxted in 1961 with coaches of 1935 and 1930 vintage, converted into a push-pull set in 1959. In 1986, the station house was boarded up but the station and signal cabin on the platform were manned during the peak hours. (P. Hay)

COWDEN

1896

Cowden Station

19. Looking towards Ashurst, we can observe some typical LBSCR features – the round ended wagon and the tapered signal post with lamp separate from the arm. The goods yard ceased to be used in 1960.
(M.G. Joly Collection)

Cowden Station, L. B. & S.C.R.

20. A postcard view reveals some decay in the platform brickwork – minor when compared with the later total loss of the canopies – a fate also suffered at Hever. This rural station is over a mile from the village of Cowden. (Lens of Sutton)

21. An economy measure introduced by the SR at many of the smaller stations featured in this album was the removal of the lever frame from the signal box to the platform, so that only one man was required. (Lens of Sutton)

1924

TONBRIDGE JUNCTION, TUNBRIDGE WELLS WEST, LEWES, and BRIGHTON.—Southern.

Miles	Down.		Week Days.																
			mrn	mrn	mrn	mrn	mrn	mrn	mrn	mrn	mrn	aft	aft	aft	aft	aft	aft (Except Saturdays)	aft	aft	aft
—	Tonbridge Junction	dep.			6 47	8 46							12 53	2e0			2 48			4e44
4¼	Tunbridge Wells Central				7 1	9 5							1 5	2e12			3 0			4e56
5¼	Tunbridge Wells West	arr.			7 10	9 14							1 12	2e18			3 5			5e2
		dep.	6 57	7 35	7 50	9 20	1020		11 5	11 15	12 5		2 0	2 35	3 0			4 5	4 25	5 5
6¼	High Rocks Halt													2 38				4 8		5 8
8¼	Groombridge	arr.	7 3	7 40	7 55	9 26	1025		1111	11 20	1211		2 7	2 41	3 8			4 12	4 31	5 11
—	218 Victoria	dep.	5 30			6 37		8 55			H1115		11 55					2 25	3H45	
—	218 London Bridge	"	5 18				8 7					s	12A20	12s50	1 38			2Y10		
—	Groombridge	dep.	7 4	7 41	7 56	9 27	1026		1112	11 21	1212		2 8	2 42	3 9			4 13	4 32	5 12
10¾	Eridge		7 18	7 47	8 1	9 32	1032	10 22	1118	11 27	1227		2 15	2 47	3 15			4 19	4 43	5 17
14¾	Crowborough & Jarvis Brook		7 27	7 55	8 9	9 40	1041	10 30		11 36	1236		2 24	2 55	3 23			4 27	4 52	5 25
19	Buxted		7 37	8 5	8 20		1053	10 39		11 46	1246	1 45	2 34		3 33				5 3	5 35
21½	Uckfield		7 44	8 10	8 27	9 54	1059	10 44		11 53	1252	1 50	2 42		3 39	3 50			5 11	5 40
24	Isfield		7 50		8 35		11 5			11 59		1 56	2 48			3 54			5 22	
26	Barcombe Mills*		7 56		8 42		1111			12 5		2 2	2 54			3 59			5 32	
29¾	Lewes 198, 204	arr.	8 4		8 49	10 9	1119			12 14		2 10	3 2			4 9			5 43	
		dep.	8 7		8 53	1010	1121			12 16		2 11	3 5			4 33			5 49	
34¾	Falmer	[244	8 19							12 28		2 22	3 15			4 43			5 59	
37	London Rd. (Brighton)	[216,	8 26		9 9		1136			12 35		2 29	3 22			4 49			6 6	
37¾	Brighton (Central) 210,	arr.	8 30		9 13	1027	1140			12 40		2 33	3 26			4 53			6 10	

Down.		Week Days—Continued.										Sundays.									
		aft (Except Saturdays)	aft	aft	aft	aft (Except Saturdays)	aft	aft (Except Saturdays)	aft	aft	aft	mrn	mrn	mrn	mrn	aft	aft	aft	aft	aft	aft
Tonbridge Junction	dep.		5e21		6s8				7 45		1157										
Tunbridge Wells Central			5e33		6s20				7 58		12 7										
Tunbridge Wells West	arr.		5e39		6s25				8 4		1212										
	dep.		5 50		6 38	6 58	7 35		9 0	9 32		7 5	7 45	9 40		1 25	3 42	4 45	7 25	8 50	
High Rocks Halt																					
Groombridge	arr.		5 53		6 46	7 3	7 42		9 5	9 39		7 10	7 50	9 45		1 30	3 47	4 50	7 30	8 57	
218 Victoria	dep.			4H50	5 5	6H6	6 6		8H5	8 5					8H50		1 14	2 30		7 5	
218 London Bridge	"	4H44		4e44	5 21	6J8	6 8		8 10	8 10					8 30		1 10			6 46	
Groombridge	dep.		5 56		6 47	7 4	7 43		9 6	9 40		7 11	7 51	9 46		1 31	3 48	4 51	7 31	8 58	
Eridge		5 46	6 2	6 12	6 53	7 14	7 49		9 15	9 47		7 17	7 56	9 51	10 13	1 36	3 54	4 58	7 37	9 4	
Crowborough & Jarvis Brook		5 54		6 21	7 1	7 22	7 57		9 21	9 55		7 26	8 4		10 22	1 44	4 8	5 8	7 46	9 14	
Buxted		6 4		6 31	7 11	7 32	8 7		9 31	10 5		7 37			10 33		4 13	5 20	7 56	9 24	
Uckfield		6 9		6 38	7 17	7 37	8 13	9 18	9 36	1012		7 44			10Z49	1 56	4 19	5 27	8 3	9 30	10 0
Isfield				6 44	7 23		8 19	9 22		1018		7 51			10 56			5 35	8 9		10 5
Barcombe Mills*				6 50	7 29		8 25	9 27		1024		7 59			11 3	2 6		5 44	8 15		1011
Lewes 198, 204	arr.			6 59	7 39		8 33	9 37		1033		8 8			11 12	2 14		5 53	8 24		1020
	dep.			7 0	7 41		8 37	9 55		1039		8 22			11 14	2 15		5 55	8 26		1025
Falmer	[244			7 10	7 53		8 49	10 5				8 34						6 7	8 37		
London Rd. (Brighton)	[216,			7 16	8 0		8 56	1011		1054		8 42			11 29	2 29		6 16	8 44		1039
Brighton (Central) 210,	arr.			7 20	8 5		9 0	1015		1059		8 46			11 34	2 33		6 21	8 48		1044

A High Level Station. Leaves Cannon Street at 12 16 aft. on Saturdays. e Except Saturdays. H Through Train to Uckfield Line Stations. J Passengers with hand luggage may change at East Croydon into the 6 6 aft. from Victoria. s Saturdays only. Y Leaves London Bridge at 2 30 aft. on Saturdays. Z Arrives Uckfield at 10 39 mrn.

* Nearly 1¼ miles to Barcombe Station.

22. Mark Beech tunnel is nearly 3/4 mile long and its southern portal was at the end of the now deserted goods yard, closed in 1960. No. 42105 bursts forth on 17th April 1954, bound for Tunbridge Wells. The white patch on the wing wall was to assist in sighting the Up Outer Home signal and van no. 11985 of 1904 was used by the S&T dept. (R.C. Riley)

BRIGHTON, LEWES, TUNBRIDGE WELLS WEST, and TONBRIDGE JUNCTION.—Southern.

Miles	Up.	Week Days. mrn	mrn	mrn	mrn	mrn	mrn	mrn	mrn	aft	aft	aft	aft	aft	aft	aft	aft	aft	aft	aft	aft
	Brighton (Central) dep.	6 55	....	8 5	9 22	10 20	....	11 5	1158		1242		....	1 38	....		2 56	....		....	....
¾	London Road (Brighton)	6 58	....	8 8	9 26	10 23	....	11 9	12 2		1245		....	1 42	....		2 59	....		....	....
3¾	Falmer	....	....	....	....	10 30	....	....	1210	Saturdays only.	1252		....	....	....		3 5	....		....	....
8	**Lewes** arr.	7 13	....	8 24	9 41	10 40	....	11 24	1222		1 2	Except Saturdays.	....	1 53	....	Except Saturdays.	3 15	....	Except Saturdays.	....	....
	Lewes dep.	7 15	....	8 26	9 42	10 41	....	11 26	1223		1 4		....	2 0	....		3 25	....		....	....
11¾	Barcombe Mills*	7 24	....	8 35	9 51	....	....	11 34	1231		1 11		....	2 9	....		3 34	....		....	....
13¾	Isfield	7 31	....	8 41	9 57	....	....	11 40	1237		1 17		....	2 15	....		3 40	....			....
16¾	Uckfield	7 37	8 35	8 49	10 4	10 56	1120	11 47	1244		1 23		1 42	2 22	....		3 46	....			4 35
18¾	Buxted	7 44	8 40	8 56	10 10	11 2	1125	11 53	1250		1 29		1 47	2 28	....		....	....			4 40
23¾	Crowborough & Jarvis Brook	7 58	8 51	9 10	10 23	11 14	1136	12 4	1 3		....		1 58	2 39	3 5		....	4 32		Except Saturdays.	4 52
27	Eridge 220, 223	8U14	8 58	9U25	10 31	11U30	1145	12U22	1 11		....		2U20	2 46	3 12		....	4 40			5 0
29	Groombridge 220 arr.	8 19	....	9 30	10 36	11 35	1149	12 27	1 17		....		2 26	2 52	3 16		....	4 46			....
63¾	220 London Bridge arr.	9 33	10B8	10 47	12 21	....	....	....	3 3	....	....	....	....	....	5 30	....	....	....	....		....
63¾	220 Victoria "	9B42	1014	10B20	....	12B38	....	....	....	....	....	....	3 41	....	....	....	....	....	....		6B29
—	Groombridge dep.	8 20	....	9 31	10 37	11 36	1150	12 28	1 18	....	....	....	2 27	2 53	3 17	....	....	4 47	....		....
31¼	High Rocks Halt	....	....	....	....	....	....	....	....	....	....	....	....	....	3 21	....	....	4 52	....		....
32	**Tunbridge Wells West** arr.	8 27	....	9 38	10 44	11 44	1157	12 35	1 25	....	....	....	2 34	3 0	3 25	....	....	4 56	....		....
	Tunbridge Wells West dep.	....	....	9 43	....	....	....	....	1 40	1 56	....	2 25	....	....	....	3 26	....	....	5 18	6 4	....
33	**Tunbridge Wells Central**	....	....	9 49	....	....	....	....	1 46	2 0	....	2 31	....	....	....	3 32	....	....	5 24	6 10	....
37¾	**Tonbridge** Junction 250 arr.	....	....	9 58	....	....	....	....	1 56	....	....	2 42	....	....	....	3 41	....	....	5 35	6 21	....

Up.	Week Days—*Continued.* aft	aft	aft	aft	aft	aft	aft	aft	aft	aft	aft	aft		Sundays. mrn	mrn	aft	aft	aft	aft	aft	aft	
Brighton (Central) dep.	4 27	....	....	5 42		6 19		7 20	7 56	....	9 5	1120	....	....	9 40	2 10	....	7 15	8 25	9 5	9 30	....
London Road (Brighton)	4 31	....	....	5 45		6 23		7 23	8 0	....	9 9	1124	....	....	9 44	2 13	....	7 19	8 29	9 8	9 33	....
Falmer	....		....	5 52	Except Saturdays.	6 30	Except Saturdays.	7 30	8 8	....	9 16	....	....	....	9 51	2 20	....	....	8 36	9 15	....	....
Lewes arr.	4 46	Runs 4 mins. later on Saturdays.	....	6 1		6 40		7 40	8 18	....	9 26	1139	....	....	10 1	2 31	....	7 34	8 46	9 25	9 48	....
Lewes dep.	4 49		....	6 2		6 50		7 42	....	8 50	9 37	1140	....	....	10 3	2 32	....	7 37	8 49	9 26	9 49	....
Barcombe Mills*	4 58		....	6 10		6 58		7 52	....	8 58	9 45	1148	....	....	1012	2 41	....	7 46	8 53	9 35	....	....
Isfield	5 4		....	6 16		7 4		7 58	....	9 4	9 51	1154	....	....	1018	2 47	....	7 52	9 4	9 41	....	....
Uckfield	5 11		5 50	6 23	6 40	7 11	7 45	8 5	....	9 10	9 57	12 0	....	....	1025	2 55	4 27	7 59	9 10	9 47	10 2	....
Buxted	5 17		5 55	6 29	6 44	7 17	7 49	8 11	....	9s16	10 4		....	....	1031	3 1	4 32	8 5	9 16	....	....	....
Crowborough & Jarvis Brook	5 30		6 6	6 41	6 55	7 30	7 59	8 24	....	9s27	1016	Wednesdays only.	....	8 12	1043	3 12	4 43	8 18	9 28	....	1015	....
Eridge 220, 223	5 38		6 16	6 50	7 3	7 38	8 6	8 33	....	9s35	1023		....	8 19	1051	3 20	4 51	8 25	9 36	....	1022	....
Groombridge 220 arr.	5 44		6 22	6 55	7 8	7 44	8 10	8 39	....	9s40	1028		....	8 24	1058	3 25	4 56	....	9 41	....	1028	....
220 London Bridge arr.	....		7 53	....	....	....	....	1016	....	....	....		....	1018	....	....	....	....	....	....	....	....
220 Victoria "	....		8 27	....	....	....	....	1010	....	....	....		....	1020	1 41	....	6 34	9B47	....	....	....	....
Groombridge dep.	5 45	....	6 23	6 56	7 9	7 45	8 11	8 40	....	9s41	1029		....	8 25	1059	3 26	4 57	....	9 42	....	1029	....
High Rocks Halt	....	....	8 27	....	....	....	....	....	....	....	....		....	....	....	....	....	....	....	....	....	....
Tunbridge Wells West arr.	5 52	....	6 31	7 8	7 16	7 52	8 18	8 47	....	9s48	1036		....	8 32	11 6	3 33	5 5	....	9 49	....	1036	....
Tunbridge Wells West dep.	....	6 25	....	....	....	....	....	9 5	....	....	....		....	....	....	....	....	....	....	....	....	....
Tunbridge Wells Central	....	6 31	....	....	....	....	....	9 10	....	....	....		....	....	....	....	....	....	....	....	....	....
Tonbridge Junction 250 arr.	....	6 42	....	....	....	....	....	9 21	....	....	....		....	....	....	....	....	....	....	....	....	....

B Through Trains from Uckfield Line Stations.
s Saturdays only.
U Arrives Eridge at 8 6, 9 18, and 11 22 mrn., 12 12 and 2 6 aft. respectively.
* Nearly 1½ miles to Barcombe Station.

For **LOCAL TRAINS** between Tonbridge Junction and Tunbridge Wells Central, see page 270.

For **OTHER TRAINS** between Tunbridge Wells West and Groombridge, see page 220; between Tunbridge Wells West and Eridge, see page 223; between Lewes and Brighton, see pages 204 and 222.

ASHURST

23. Traffic here has always been relatively light as the district is thinly populated. These three photographs were taken on 17th April 1954 and this south facing one shows a glazed panel erected to give some protection to the operator of the lever frame. Today only the nearby brick shed remains standing. (D. Cullum)

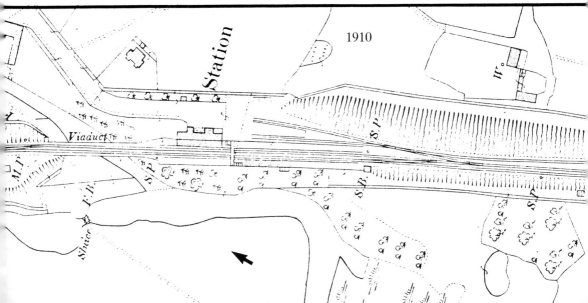

24. The garden-style seat on the up platform backed onto the tranquil river and, after the departure of the motor train, it was well placed to view the down platform rockery. The viaduct beyond the locomotive crossed over the mill stream – England's green and pleasant land indeed. (D. Cullum)

25. In the early evening, for over 20 years, there was a period of notable activity. The 4.50 pm Victoria to Brighton train would call at 6.00 pm and after its departure the train seen here would move into the platform to collect passengers changing for Groombridge and Tunbridge Wells West. (R.C. Riley)

26. A photograph taken at the same time of day on 5th June 1962, shows that passengers no longer had to change. No. 80065 departs with the Brighton portion at 6.2 whilst U1 class no. 31909 waits in the goods yard to take the remaining three coaches on to Tunbridge Wells at 6.8. (S.C. Nash)

London Brighton & South Coast Railway.

Heathfield to

CHELSEA

27. The triangular junction was controlled by three signal boxes – Ashurst Junction in the west; Groombridge Junction in the east and Birchden Junction in the south. Here we look out from Ashurst Junction box towards Ashurst and see the single line to East Grinstead branching off to the left. (D. Cullum)

28. Looking in the opposite direction, the 12.45 from Tunbridge Wells West comes into view on 19th April 1954. (D. Cullum)

29. For many years after its construction, the line between Ashurst and Birchden Junctions was only used for the storage of locomotives awaiting repair or scrapping. Local birds soon found them ideal nest locations. Eventually the line was doubled and opened to through traffic on 7th June 1914. (S.C. Nash Collection)

2. Lewes to Crowborough
LEWES

A few lines from Lewes.

30. A corny postcard shows class D1 no. 257 formerly *Brading*, on the Uckfield line and the Eastbourne lines on the right. Between them is the less obvious turntable – only the buffers beyond it show. (Lens of Sutton)

> The fascinating story of the development of this station is told, with the aid of many maps and photographs, in our *Haywards Heath to Seaford* and *Brighton to Eastbourne* albums.

London Brighton and South Coast Railway

———

Buxted to

Emsworth

31. This is the signalman's outlook in 1956 – the 9.00am Brighton to Tonbridge service leaves behind class L no. 31778 whilst class C2X no. 32536 waits in the up Brighton loop (it will later depart with a single coach for East Grinstead) and a stopping train from Haywards Heath stands in the down London platform. (P. Hay)

32. One of the popular U class rumbles over Every's Bridge on 12th November 1950, as it approaches Lewes with the 8.50 am Victoria to Brighton via Uckfield. This area has been totally transformed by the Lewes bypass. (S.C. Nash)

33. Sleeches Viaduct took the line over the River Ouse and was built in 1868 when the route was diverted from its original course south of Hamsey. Class U1 no. 31910 hauls the 2.55 pm Brighton to Tonbridge train north on 18th April 1960. (S.C. Nash)

34. About three miles north of Lewes, the single line to East Grinstead diverged at Culver Junction. Part of this route is now the Bluebell Railway. No. 80032 hurries south, with a Victoria to Brighton train on 3rd July 1954, passing the very short siding which houses a platelayer's trolley. About once a year, a truck of coal would be delivered here to supply the signal box stove. (D. Cullum)

London Brighton and South Coast Railway.

Hartfield to

Bosham

35. On 5th July 1923, D1 class no. 253 came to grief north of the junction due to deformation of the track expanded by the hot weather. The train was the 4.27 pm Brighton to Tunbridge Wells and the only injuries were bruises on the driver. (A.B. MacLeod)

BRIGHTON, LEWES, UCKFIELD, GROOMBRIDGE, and TUNBRIDGE WELLS.—London, Brighton, and South Coast.

BARCOMBE MILLS

36. The original 1858 buildings were extended in about 1900 but it does not appear that a footbridge was ever provided. The down platform on the right was close to the River Ouse which is prone to flood in this area. (Lens of Sutton)

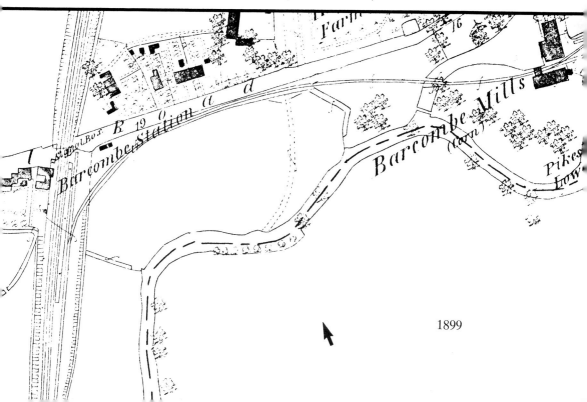

1899

37. The clear exhaust must be admired as L class no. 31777 accelerates southwards in September 1957, bound for Brighton. Unlike most closed stations, it has now been impeccably restored to look like railway premises, although devoid of track. (P. Hay)

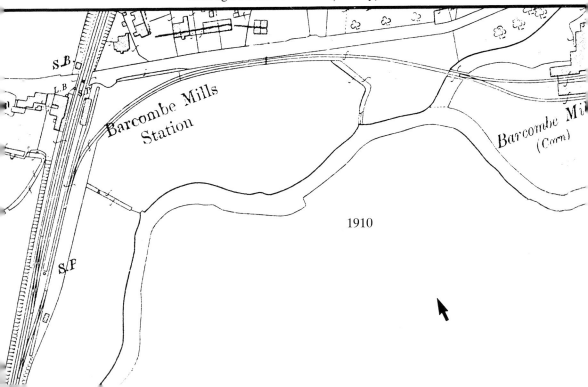

38. The line had been scheduled for closure on 6th January 1969 but, owing to formalities regarding the replacement bus service, it was delayed. In the meantime a defective bridge near Lewes was discovered and single line working was ordered. A shuttle service was run – 2H no. 1120 is seen operating it whilst 3D no. 1318 has just terminated from Oxted, on 22nd February, two days before services were withdrawn. (S.C. Nash)

The 1899 edition shows another mill siding half way between Barcombe Mills and Isfield stations.

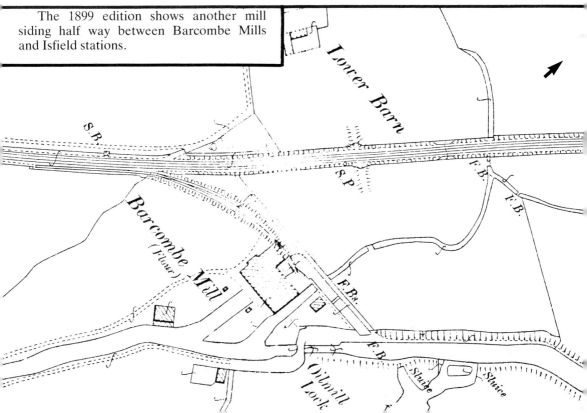

39. The station was a mirror image of the one at Barcombe Mills and had been similarly extended at the same time. Cessation of train services did not mean closure of the booking office – tickets for use on the bus were issued there for some time. (Lens of Sutton)

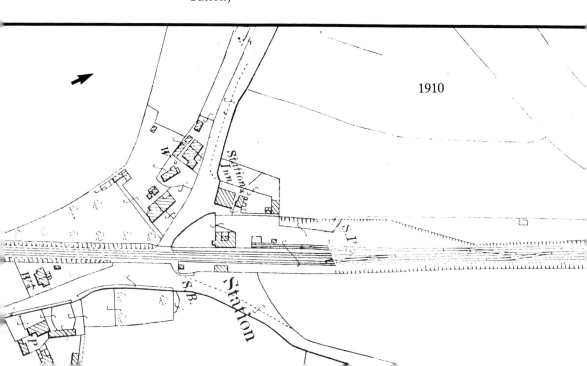

1910

40. A view from the 1930s shows class I3 no. 2029 southbound with a Brighton train composed of an ex-SECR set with birdcage look-outs each end. Who could have imagined that in 1984 the station would be restored; track relaid and steam trains would be running again, if only for a short distance. The "Lavender Line" has been created by the Milham family and was named after the coal merchant who still used the station yard. (Dr. I.C. Allen)

BEST RESTORED
STATION 1985

ANNIE 1904 0-4-0
SADDLE TANK
ANDREW BARCLAY.
Built in Kilmarnock it was used as a shunting engine by Yeates and Duxbury Papermills in Manchester until 1973.

SAPPHIRE
THE PULLMAN COACH
Built in 1910 by the Birmingham Railway Carriage & Wagon Co. as a 24 seater first class car for The Pullman Car Co. In 1953 it was used by the Queen for the Spithead Coronation Naval Review. It is the oldest Pullman car on wheels in this country.

STEVENSON
HAWTHORNE 0-6-0
UGLY CLASS No.62.
was built for Corby Steel works in 1950 and was in constant use until the closure of the works.

as, fourteen years after the last ticket was punched, that British put the For Sale sign up at Isfield Station.

ven and Dave Milham went to the auction out of pure curiosity, ame away owning a slice of railway history.

ter the bubbling excitement of the auction room came the harsh ty. The new station master and his wife took a tour of the lings. What they saw was not exactly a romantic scene out of the way Children. It was an overgrown ruin in a total state srepair.

David said: "We just had to roll our sleeves up and get on with it. But the whole family mucked in and within a few weeks we had cleared the trees off the track, and things snowballed from there."

Today Isfield Station is looking better than it has done for a good many years, tastefully restored with loving care to its former glory.

Everything's been done in Southern Railway colours - from the signal box to the ladies loo - and it is easy to believe that this was the way it looked when the station first opened

UCKFIELD

41. In these days of staff reductions it is easy to forget the normal staffing levels of a reasonably important country station. (M.G. Joly Collection)

42. The original terminal buildings were replaced in 1901 by this handsome double-gabled structure and a lengthy canopy was provided over the up platform. The road transport of the era is worthy of close examination. (Lens of Sutton)

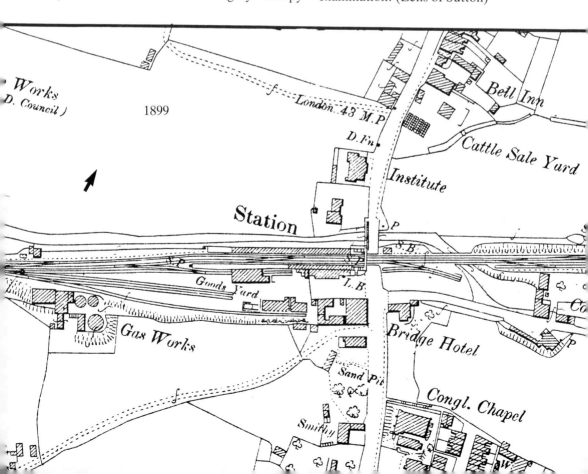

43. Heavy rain on 25th July 1931 seems to have flooded the shed road again. The goods shed had doors at the other end (see picture No. 41) so that empty wagons could be pushed out. The inconvenient crossover between the platforms was replaced by two at opposite ends of the station. They are visible in the next two pictures. (Late E. Wallis)

44. Class H2 no. 32421 passes over the south crossover in June 1955, with a train destined for Brighton. The crossover was still in use over thirty years later, being used by terminating DEMUs. (S.C. Nash)

45. The leading coach of the 12.10 from Tonbridge is on the bridge over the river, which then turns to pass behind the signal box and up platform. The locomotive is 2–6–4T no. 88032 and the date is 11th July 1958. This is the site, advocated by many, for a new terminus, which would eliminate the level crossing. (D. Cullum)

47. In 1985, the station was becoming a museum piece, with three semaphore signals in view and gates operated by a wheel. All trains still arrived at the down platform and departed from the up. (J. Scrace)

46. Cameras were out in profusion on 11th May 1984 to record the last regular locomotive hauled London service, headed by no. 33107. The down line had become a headshunt and the goods yard, a bus park. (P. Barnes)

BUXTED

48. The population served by this small country station has increased modestly and includes Hadlow Down and Maresfield.
(Lens of Sutton)

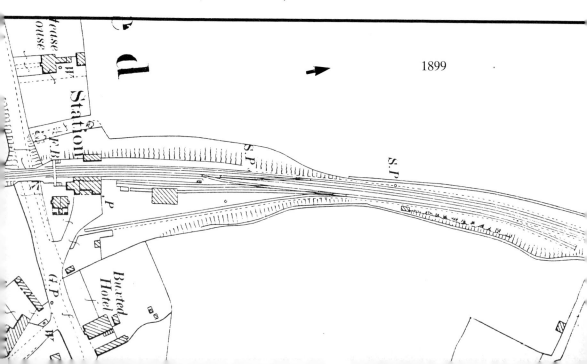

1899

49. Peace returns on 1st September 1953, as the up train starts its climb to Rotherfield Tunnel in the heights of Ashdown Forest in the background. (R.C. Riley)

50. Apart from the loss of the signal box and the canopy of the down platform (on the left), little has changed in nearly 20 years since this photograph was taken in 1958. (D. Cullum)

51. Standard class 4 no. 80031 winds its way south on 20th April 1960, with a set of "plum and custard" coaches. There was no better way of feasting one's eyes on the Sussex countryside than from these. (S.C. Nash)

52. On 5th April 1916, D1 tank no. 273 was descending the 1 in 66 gradient near Burnt Oak Bridge when it mysteriously left the rails. Driver Paige emerged "scratched and much annoyed" whilst the Inspecting Officer declared "some weakness in the line" to be responsible. Fireman Savage found himself sitting in the cab roof. (S. Page Mitchell).

CROWBOROUGH

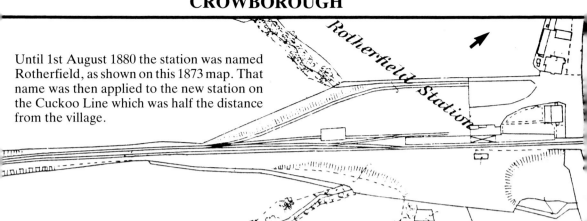

Until 1st August 1880 the station was named Rotherfield, as shown on this 1873 map. That name was then applied to the new station on the Cuckoo Line which was half the distance from the village.

53. The station was substantially rebuilt in 1905–07 and this view shows the new spacious up platform. Photograph no. 90 in *Steaming* *through East Sussex* (Middleton Press) illustrates the original building. (Lens of Sutton)

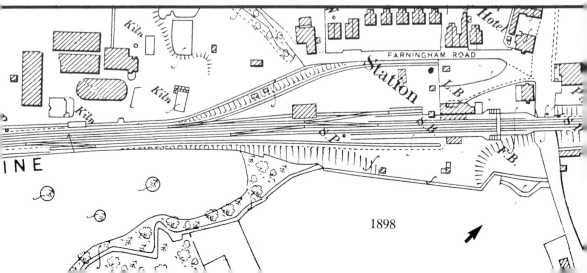

1898

54. During World War I, there were up to 28000 troops at Crowborough Camp, and their transport, together with their equipment and supplies, placed an immense strain on railway resources. A partial solution was to remove some of the fence to the goods yard and extend the back siding in front of the station. Stationmaster Reddish was awarded the MBE for his efforts. (B.C. Vigor Collection)

55. Looking east across the 1907 goods yard in 1924, the variety of wagons and profusion of coal merchants signs is noticeable. Ten sidings were provided on this side of the line, in addition to the original two on the up side. (B.C. Vigor)

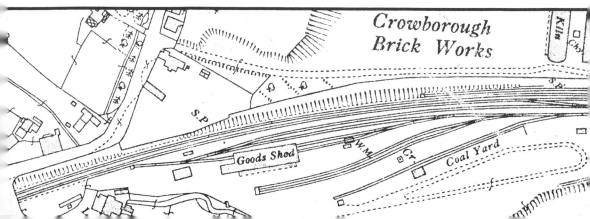

56. The spaciousness of the facilities is evident in this 1953 photograph of the 2.2 pm Tunbridge Wells West-Lewes train. Jarvis Brook was added to the station name in 1897. (R.C. Riley)

Bertram Vigor recalls.....

CROWBOROUGH — TUNBRIDGE WELLS 1916-1921

Getting to school entailed catching the 8.05 am from Crowborough six days a week, but before describing the train let us move on to the next station, Eridge, to see what was already occurring there. The first train up the "Cuckoo Line" from Eastbourne would already have arrived and it comprised through carriages for Victoria and Tunbridge Wells, the latter the rear portion. The engine, as often as not, was D1 tank No 298 or 362, but others such as I2 tank No 19, I3 tank No 88 or even a B2X 4-4-0 No 209 would take their turn. On arrival at Eridge the engine was detached drawn forward and run via the down main and crossover to be attached to the rear of the train at the up loop platform. Meanwhile the Victoria coaches were uncoupled from the Tunbridge Wells portion. By now the Brighton train — 8.05 from Crowborough would be due, comprising through coaches for London Bridge and Tunbridge Wells, with at the head a "Gladstone", a B2X 4-4-0 or a B4 4-4-0, an I3 tank or on occasion an H Atlantic. Of this selection B4 No 50 sticks out in the memory as being a regular, H No 39 *La France* 13 class No 27 whose whistle suffered from chronic laryngitis, and No 213 *Bessemer* a 4-4-0 of class B3X joining in as required. Surely every Brighton based engine, of those classes must have worked that train during my 5½ years stint. To return to Eridge, however, the sequences of operations was now:-

(1) Brighton up train is divided and front portion draws forward on the up main and then sets back to the up loop to be coupled to the Victoria coaches.

(2) Eastbourne loco shunts through Tunbridge Wells coaches from up loop to up main where they are coupled to the coaches from Brighton.

(3) Combined London Bridge and Victoria train departs from up loop platform, only

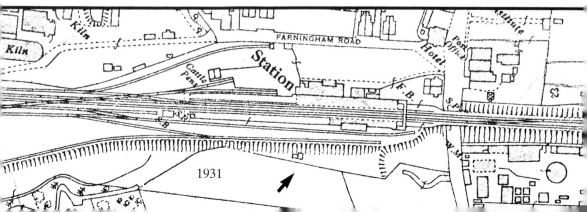

1931

to be split again into constituents at East Croydon for final distribution.

(4) Eastbourne engine attains the head of the Tunbridge Wells train by following the London train through the up loop and finally setting back.

(5) The London train having cleared Birchden Junction, the Tunbridge Wells train departs and peace once again descends upon Eridge. Just over one hour later similar moves were re-enacted, the one minor difference being that the through carriages from the Brighton and Eastbourne lines ran non-stop to Victoria. Less complicated shunts also occurred between 11 and 11.30am and again round about 2pm, but thereafter the interesting moves were associated with the down platforms.

Journeys home from school did not involve any particular train, as Wednesdays and Saturdays were half days. On other days we usually caught the 4.21 pm from Tunbridge Wells, actually a "Cuckoo Line" train, from which we had to change at Eridge, and to complete our journey by no less a train than the 3.45 pm from Victoria, first stop Eridge. The 3.45 was quite a train, for it slipped a van and two coaches at Ashurst for Tunbridge Wells and then divided at Eridge — a van and three coaches for Brighton and two coaches and a van for Eastbourne, the latter taken forward by the 4.21 pm ex Tunbridge Wells. The engine on the 3.45 was usually a Gladstone, with the occasional Atlantic. No 39, *La France* covered the 3.5 miles from Eridge to Crowborough in 5 mins 20 secs start to stop, climbing all the way with some 2 miles at 1 in 80. On Saturdays the 3.45 was almost exclusively an I3 turn. Other trains home were the 4.05 pm and the 5.05 pm, both Terrier-hauled Balloon control trailers. The 4.05 terminated at Crowborough at 4.27, returned to Tunbridge Wells at 4.32 and then formed the 5.05 to Uckfield. Two of the Terriers shared the duty — numbers 667 and 677. In 1917 both left the area for work of national importance and their duties were taken over by two D1 tanks, numbers 266 and 275.

As the war dragged on the position regarding rolling stock repair became acute and all sorts of pensioned rolling stock returned to active service. The 2.00 from Tunbridge Wells often included Stroudley four wheel coaches, austere in the extreme as regards comfort. The only relief on the boarded partitions was an advertisement imploring Londoners to "Live in the Country", and the Stroudley-Rusbridge passenger communication knob. On occasion the 4.21 would shrink to one 48 ft composite coach and a six wheel guards van, bursting at the seams until the Brighton line passengers detrained at Eridge. It was fortunate that we did not have to attend school on Sundays as the train service was meagre in the extreme — the first up train did not depart until 10.43. However, on one Sunday during the Summer there would be one additional train — the Hay Train, comprising an E, tank, two or three open wagons and a brake van. It job was to collect the crop of hay from embankments and cuttings, from which it had previously been cut, dried and raked into large heaps at points convenient for loading. One assumes that the railway horses benefitted!

(Reproduced from Bluebell News)

58. Owing to their infrequency, weed killing trains are an uncommon photographic subject. Q class no. 30545 propels its train of semi- retired tenders towards Redgate Mill Junction on 17th September 1951. (A.F. Mercer)

59. Redgate Mill Junction is the point at which the single line from Hailsham joined the double track from Uckfield, 1¼ miles south of Eridge. When the latter route was single, the two lines ran parallel to Eridge. (D. Cullum)

57. Nearly ½ mile south of the station, Tunnel Bridge spans the line. This northward view from it shows the second and larger goods shed, as the 5.10pm Tonbridge to Brighton runs toward Rotherfield Tunnel. 2–6–4T no. 80154 was the last steam engine built at Brighton Works. (D. Cullum)

3. Polegate to
Tunbridge Wells West
POLEGATE

60. The Hailsham branch originally faced towards Lewes but in 1880–81 it was redirected to allow through running to Eastbourne necessitating a new station further east. This is described as Swines Hill Bridge but after the new station opened it carried "Station Road". Half way to Hailsham, a trailing branch on the west side of the line ran to the works of the Maidenhead Brick & Tile Co. (P. Pannett Collection)

62. The 5.44pm (Saturdays only) Eastbourne to Tunbridge Wells West bears against the check rail on leaving the junction on 1st June 1957. Maps and photograph nos. 87 to 99 in our *Brighton to Eastbourne* album expand the story of the interesting station. (P. Hay)

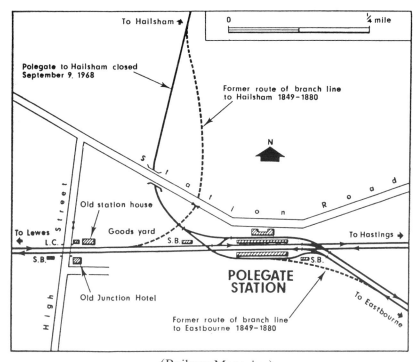

(Railway Magazine)

61. The new station comprised two island platforms with the main buildings at the lower street level – the roof is just visible. On 25th May 1986 a new station was opened on the site of the first one, close to the level crossing and more convenient for the High Street. The train in the loop is signalled for Hailsham whilst the main line train displays the headcode for London Bridge. (J. Harrod Collection)

HAILSHAM

63. As at Uckfield, the main buildings were on the down side and were also used as a terminus for many years, both initially and latterly. This photograph is thought to date from 1865–70 and shows the locomotive shed on the left. (R. Girling Collection)

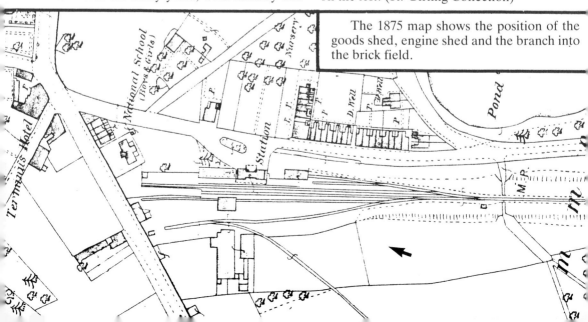

The 1875 map shows the position of the goods shed, engine shed and the branch into the brick field.

64. No. 115 was a 2–4–0T built by Sharp Stewart in 1869 and is seen by the early, rather plain, platform canopy sometime after 1874, before which it bore the no. 96. It is described in more detail in the introduction to our *Branch Line to Hayling*. (R. Girling Collection)

65. Looking from the end of the goods yard it appears that the up platform has been built but that no canopy has been erected. Services northwards commenced on 5th April 1880, as far as Heathfield, controlled by the new signal box on the left. (R. Girling Collection)

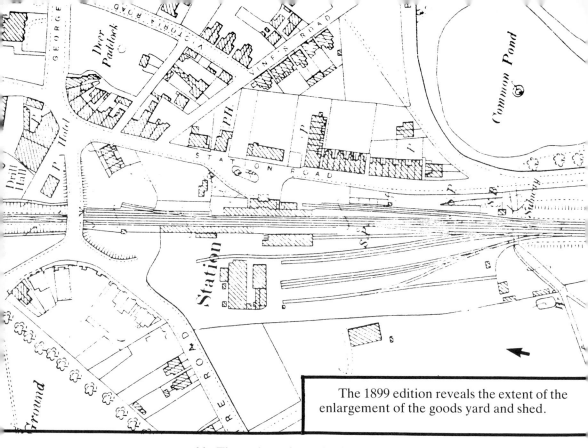

The 1899 edition reveals the extent of the enlargement of the goods yard and shed.

66. The enlarged goods shed and both the signal boxes could be seen from the road bridge. Today there is no trace of anything in this view – only the redundant bridge remains to impede road traffic. (Lens of Sutton)

67. On 8th April 1950, class J1 no. 32325 calls with the 11.8 am Victoria to Eastbourne whilst the 12.55 from Eastbourne stands in the up platform and class D3 no. 2385 stands in the bay with the push-pull set that shuttled between here and Eastbourne. (S.C. Nash)

68. No. 32475, one of the faithful class E4 0–6–2Ts, departs for Eastbourne from the up platform in June 1957. Don't miss the church and the former South Box on the right. (P. Hay)

69. North Box had long been disused when no. 80140 arrived with the 15.14 from Tunbridge Wells West on 24th May 1965, about three weeks before services from that town were withdrawn. The up line continued as a siding for some distance beyond the points. (J. Scrace)

70. By September 1968 only a DEMU unit ran to and from Eastbourne; the crane was redundant, as were the six sidings in the goods yard, which had closed in the August of that year. The down bay line had also served a dock with four cattle pens and once ran southwards into Burtenshaw and Green's private siding. (J. Scrace)

HELLINGLY

71. Until 1899 this rural station simply served the needs of the small village and the local agricultural community. But in that year, work commenced on building the massive East Sussex Asylum, as it was then called. To facilitate construction, the contractors laid down a 1¼ mile long branch from the station. (Lens of Sutton)

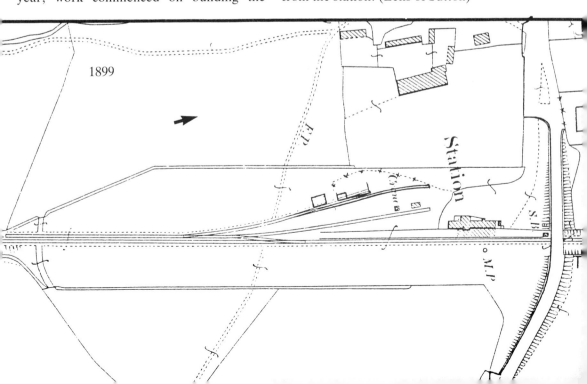

72. When the hospital opened in 1903, the County Council acquired the branch line and electrified it. This view shows the standards for the overhead wire and the island exchange platform, which appears to be roped off when not in use. (Lens of Sutton)

73. Part of the overhead equipment in the exchange sidings can be seen above the cab of the D1 on this southbound train. The electrification was at 500 volts DC, a system commonly used on contemporary tramways. (Lens of Sutton)

74. The building contractor used a steam locomotive but the County Council purchased this 14 hp machine for the line in 1903, probably from Germany. Its main purpose was to haul coal – two wagons at a time – to the hospital boilers and generators, where its own current was made. This it did until March 1959 when oil took over from coal. (S.C. Nash)

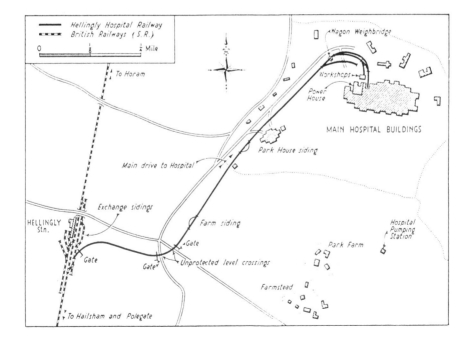

(Railway Magazine)

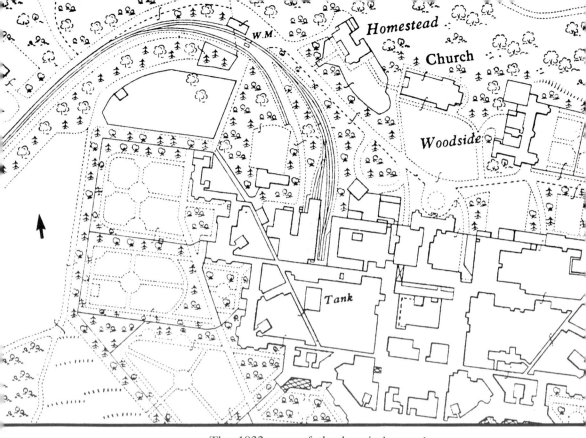

The 1932 map of the hospital complex shows a short platform for passengers at the extreme end of the line.

76. The timber island platform was removed in 1932 and by the time this photograph was taken in 1965 there was no trace of the exchange sidings. This was the only station on the line to be without passing facilities. (J. Scrace)

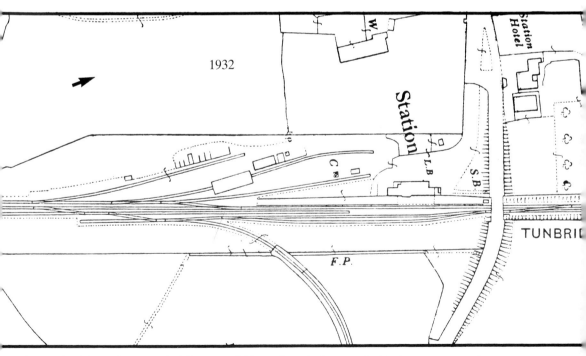

75. Until 1931 patients and visitors could be electrically hauled to the hospital in this 12-seater Brush tramcar, seen here in 1953, pensioned off as a sports pavilion in the hospital grounds. Its frame was used to make a wagon, which then doubled the line's wagon fleet. (S.C. Nash)

HORAM

77. This is one of those dithering stations with uncertainty about its name – Horeham Road for Waldron until 1891; Horeham Road & Waldron up to 1900; Waldron & Horeham Road for the next 35 years and finally Horam, plain and effective.
(P. Pannett Collection)

78. The gardener would have preferred "Horam". Taken in about 1883, we can see the oil lit coach standards of the period; the embossed plaster panels and a massive load of hay leaving the goods yard.
(P. Pannett Collection)

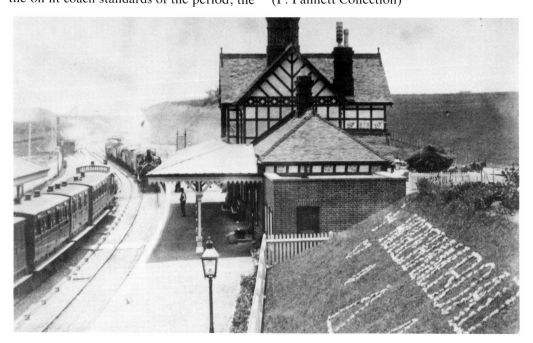

79. Lavish architecture and lavish provision of signal boxes was typical of both this line and the Midhurst – Chichester route, opened the following year. This is North Box. South Box is partly obscured by steam in the previous picture. (P. Pannett Collection)

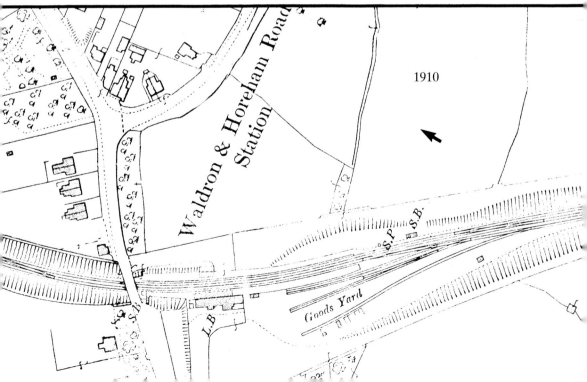

80. Lavish provisions even extended to staff foot crossings. The ornamental plasterwork gave problems with damp penetration and so this and many other similar stations were tile hung. (Lens of Sutton)

82. Two trains a day started at Heathfield in 1965 – 6.40 am and 1.40 pm. This is the latter train, two days before closure of the line. It was scheduled to wait 7 minutes at Horam. Time to lean on your shovel. (J. Scrace)

81. The crew of C class no. 31272 stop for a rest on the down platform on 1st June 1957. The lever frame is on the opposite platform – placed there when the two signal boxes were abolished. (P. Hay)

3633

SOUTHERN RAILWAY.
This ticket is issued subject to the Company's
Bye-laws, Regulations and Conditions in their
Time Tables, Notices and Book of Regulations.
Waldron & Horeham Road to
Waldron & H.Rd.   Waldron & H.Rd.
St.Leonards W.Sq.   St.Leonards W.Sq.
ST. LEONARDS WARRIOR SQ.
THIRD CLASS   THIRD CLASS
Fare 2/10   Fare 2/10

3633

HEATHFIELD

83. The coming of the railways caused rapid building development in the area – the present High Street possessed only two buildings in 1875! The goods yard was cut into the side of the hill and the station set at right angles and higher than the platform, the awnings of which can be seen beyond the fully glazed footbridge. (Lens of Sutton)

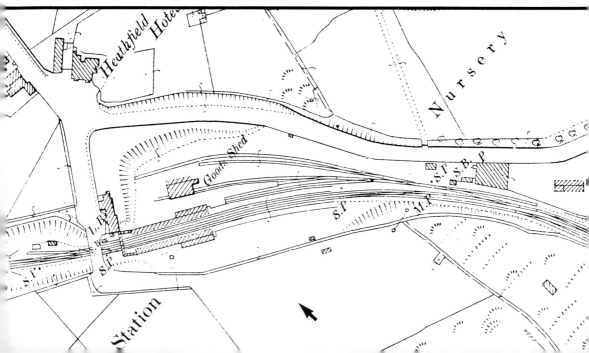

84. The Cuckoo Line takes its name from the Cuckoo Fair held at Heathfield on April 14th each year, at which event a cuckoo is released from a basket. Its first song is reputed to herald summer. The covered way leading down to the footbridge is above the chimney of no. 298. (Lens of Sutton)

85. Between the water tank and the road bridge we see two gas holders, which received natural gas from a bore hole. This was used for lighting the station; operating a gas engine for pumping the water and some was compressed into cylinders. These can be seen lying down and when sufficient were filled, the hoist on the side of the tank was used to load them into a wagon shunted into the short siding. They were sent to a laboratory specialising in testing flameproof electric motors used in mines etc.
(O.J. Morris/E.R. Lacey Collection)

86. A 1955 picture shows the siding which ran the full length of the 266yd tunnel; the single line to Mayfield; the 25ft gas siding and North Box. Part of the northern end of the tunnel has recently been transformed as a children's playground. (D. Cullum)

87. The 2.39pm Tunbridge Wells West to Eastbourne gains momentum again, as the driver of the goods relaxes at ground level and gives a friendly wave. His train was previously seen at Horam. (P. Hay)

THE DISCOVERY OF NATURAL GAS

A geological survey in 1875 reported subterranean gas but no further investigations were recorded.

In 1895, an artesian well was being drilled for the Heathfield Hotel, immediately north of the station, when the drilling fluids started to "boil." A candle was lowered to investigate with spectacular results – "a flame as high as a man". The depth was 288 ft, and as no water was found, the bore was sealed.

Apparently unaware of the lack of water, the LBSCR sunk its own well in August 1896. At 312 ft, there was a "foul smell and rushing of wind." By way of experiment, a match was applied! The flame was estimated to be 16 ft high.

The station was lit by gas from this source from 1898 and as the supply was reported to be so promising, the Natural Gas Company was formed in 1902. Its prospectus stated the venture "was going to revolutionise the industrial life of Britain." It sunk four bore holes but was not a commercial success. It was about seventy years too early and in the wrong place.

In 1963, the railway's supply was reported to be dwindling and so the bore was sealed off.

88. The signalman awaits the staff as grimy no. 80140 runs northward on 24th May 1965. The goods yard remained open for coal traffic until 26th April 1968, when a road crane damaged an under bridge near Horsebridge and precipitated total closure of the line. (J. Scrace)

89. About 2½ miles north of Heathfield, no. 297 *Bonchurch* of class D1 derailed running north on 1st September 1897. The driver was killed and there were several injuries in the wrecked coaches. Poor track and a tight timetable on the very hilly, sharply curved line were held to blame. (E.R. Lacey Collection)

London Brighton & South Coast Railway.

Rotherfield to

Chichester

90. Relief Station Master Harry Holden poses in his LBSCR frock coat whilst wearing his new SR cap, sometime in 1923. Note the LBSCR hand cart and the Refreshments signboard. (B.C. Vigor)

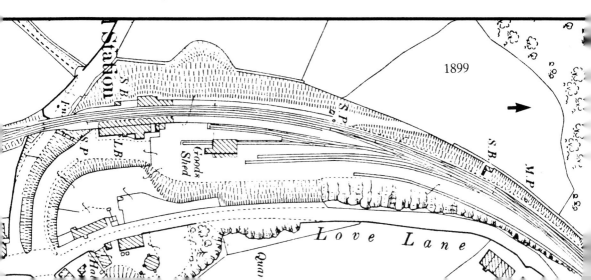

91. The Cuckoo Line from Horam to Redgate Mill Junction was an almost continuous series of reverse curves – even in the stations. The signal is off for the up train – its post was made from two former running rails. (Lens of Sutton)

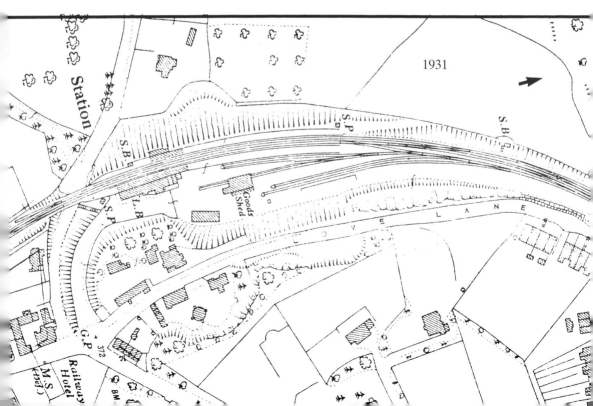

92. The architectural features are similar to those on the Bluebell line stations, including the tile hanging modification. Although the Austin and Vauxhall date from the 1930s, the photograph was in fact taken in 1955. (D. Cullum)

93. The south end of the station offered a particularly vicious catch point on the up side but a lengthy siding on the down. A flight of steps was provided for passengers needing a short cut to the station approach – its handrail is visible to the right of the bridge parapets. (D. Cullum)

ROTHERFIELD

94. The station was ¾ mile from the village and there was a 160ft climb to it. This faded postcard at least gives an impression of its rural location and the undulating countryside. (Lens of Sutton)

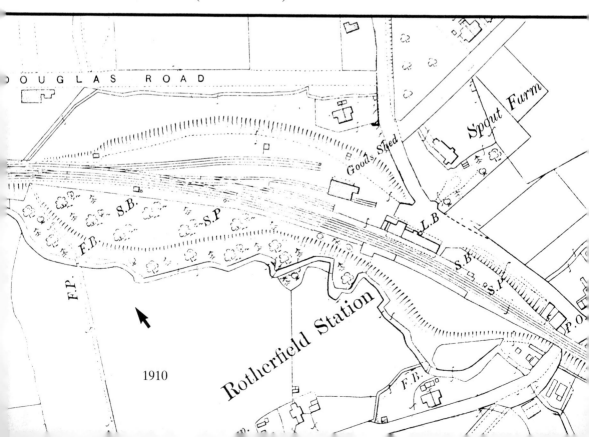

95. Side face was the rule of many Victorian photographers, which was fine in a studio but only made the subjects look fit for Madame Tussauds in an architectural photograph. At least the south-west facade is clear. (M.G. Joly Collection)

96. A wisp of steam issues from the Westinghouse air pump on the cabside and a smelly mixture emerges from the chimney, as class E5 no. 32588 arrives on 16th February 1952. Staff still only used the old LBSCR number 588 and so did not clean the prefix 32. (J.J. Smith)

97. On 19th April 1954, the goods yard was still busy with coal traffic and general merchandise. The conifers and mixed woodland gave the line a particularly attractive aura. (D. Cullum)

99. By 1965, the oil lights evident in the previous photographs had been replaced by SR-style electric ones. In the last weeks of operation, it seems that engine cleaning had ceased, judging by the state of no. 80034. (J. Scrace)

98. A closer look at the station on the same day confirms its family likeness to the others on the line. The hilly nature of the track is also evident – this combined with its incessant curvature kept average speeds fairly low. (D. Cullum)

London Brighton & South Coast Railway.

Horeham to

EastGrinstead

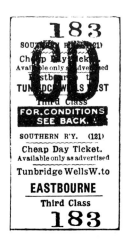

183
SOUTHERN R'Y (121)
Cheap Day Ticket
Available only as advertised
Eastbourne to
TUNDGE WELLS WEST
Third Class
FOR.CONDITIONS
SEE BACK.

SOUTHERN R'Y. (121)
Cheap Day Ticket.
Available only as advertised
Tunbridge Wells W. to
EASTBOURNE
Third Class
183

ERIDGE

100. There is no village of Eridge, the station being named after nearby Eridge Park, in which Eridge Castle is situated. Initially there was a small station on the single line to Uckfield, approached at ground level as was the first station at Burgess Hill. (D. Cullum)

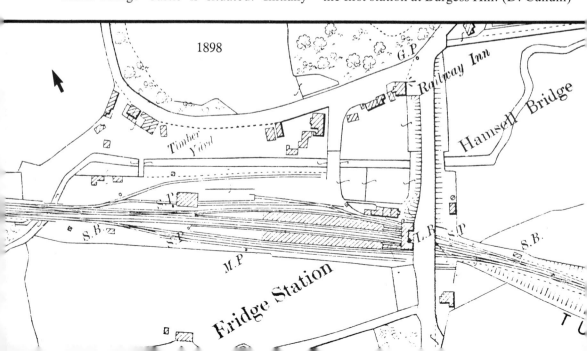

101. This station was opened in 1880 and the platforms on the left served the Heathfield line whilst the two on the right were used by trains to and from the single line to Lewes. After the doubling of the latter route, they became separate up and down platforms. An unusual feature, although not visible in this view, is a mailbag chute under the up platform staircase. (Lens of Sutton)

102. The box remained in use in 1986, although it was not as busy as when the Tonbridge service was operating. Until July 1985, the DEMUs on this service arrived at platform 4 and were crossed to platform 1 for departure. The box is seen here in 1976, flanked by an aid to beer production and an aid to its disposal. (J. Scrace)

103. Class I3 departs from platform 2 with the 4.11 pm Lewes to Victoria on August Bank Holiday 1950. The spacious goods shed seems to be in excess of any likely local traffic. (S.C. Nash)

London Brighton and South Coast Railway.

Eridge to

Lt. Hamp. Har.

104. Birchden Junction signal box controlled the divergence of the lines to Oxted (left) and Tunbridge Wells West (right). The 1.56pm departure from the latter place is seen behind class 4 2–6–4T no. 80011 on 19th April 1954. (D. Cullum)

105. Groombridge Junction box stood in equally pleasant countryside, overlooking the line to Eridge (centre) and the route to Ashurst Junction, on the right. (Lens of Sutton)

GROOMBRIDGE

106. The 1866 station was almost entirely rebuilt to create this imposing building in 1897. The slated spirelet and the poly-chromatic brickwork give the impression of an attempt to mimic Tunbridge Wells West on a smaller scale. (M.G. Joly Collection)

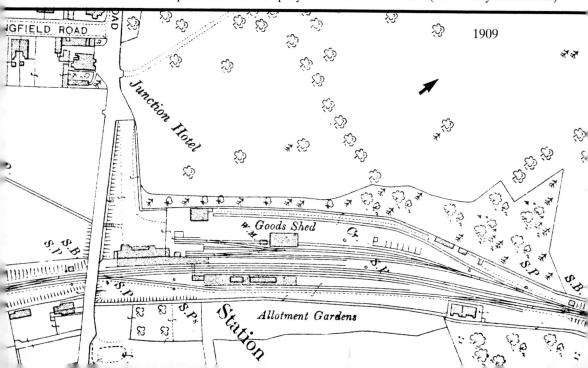

107. Before the Ashurst spur was opened, trains from London to Eastbourne had to reverse here. This service started in 1888 and here we see a class D1 tank attached to the rear of a southbound train which had arrived behind Stroudley single no. 339 *London*. (S.C. Nash Collection)

108. A shunting box was provided by the west crossover. A milk van was a common sight in passenger trains until road transport won the churn traffic. (Lens of Sutton)

109. Generous canopies were provided which were of great value when this was a junction station. The one on the up island platform was erected in 1897–98. This 1952 view shows the junction distant signals. (D. Cullum)

110. An up goods train passes the old signal box, in May 1958, whilst its replacement is under construction at the end of the down platform. (D. Cullum)

111. By 1976, the canopies and the loop line had gone although the electric lighting had been modernised. In 1985, the Tunbridge Wells and Eridge Railway Preservation Society was formed. With the unfortunate initial letters of TWERPS, it hopes to restore services eventually. (J. Scrace)

HIGH ROCKS HALT

112. The outcrops of sandstone in the area produce some spectacular scenery. A motor train halt was opened on 1st June 1907, largely for the benefit of visitors to the beautiful countryside. (M.G. Joly Collection)

113. The down platform was on the east side of the road bridge. The little used halt was closed on 5th May 1952, although it was temporarily out of use in the early years of World War II. (Lens of Sutton)

TUNBRIDGE WELLS WEST

114. Until the formation of the SR, the two stations at this spa town were differentiated as SER or LBSCR. After 22nd August 1923, they were officially Central and West respectively. The station approach is illuminated by a Jablachkoff candle, an early form of arc light. (Lens of Sutton)

115. The grandiose Victorian architecture has attracted a "listed status" which should ensure its future survival even though no trains now operate. The island platform on the left was created about 1884 but it lost its canopy nearly a century later.
(Lens of Sutton)

116. The 1.50pm to Eastbourne on 14th May 1949 was hauled by no.2253, the last active D1 on East Sussex lines at that time. Few improvements were made by BR – most of the trains continued to terminate here, over a mile from the town centre. (R.C. Riley)

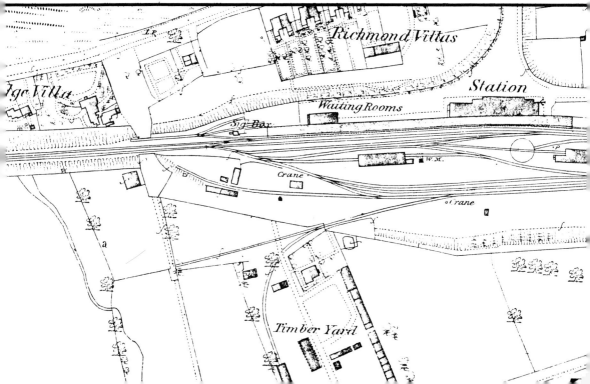

The 1883 map shows waiting rooms remote from the main station and a two-road locomotive shed to the right of the turntable.

117. The original slate roof was badly damaged by bombs on 20th November 1940 and it was eventually replaced by this asbestos structure. This 1960 view shows no. 75069 on shed – four years earlier 25 locomotives were allocated here – 3 years later none was left. (J. Scrace)

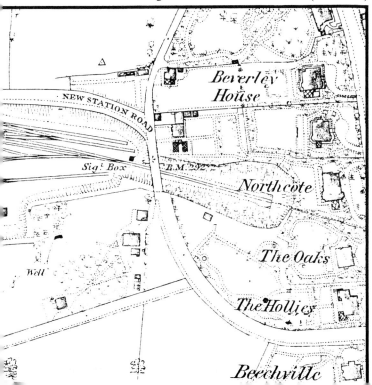

118. Empty coaches bound for New Cross Gate leave on 16th June 1963 and pass the large goods shed, which was subsequently used as a wholesale greengrocery. This location was once very busy. For example in 1956, there were 70 passenger and 5 goods trains arriving each weekday – a train movement every 8 minutes. (S.C. Nash)

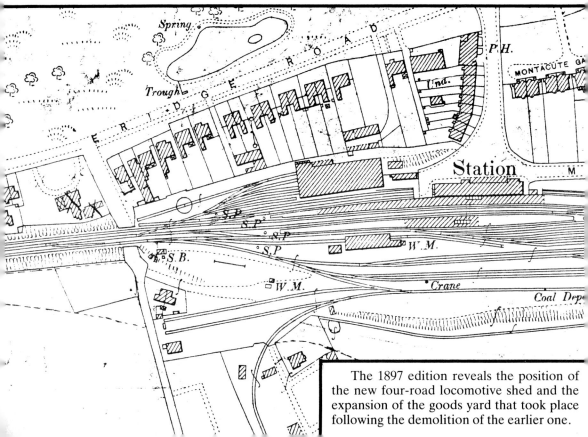

The 1897 edition reveals the position of the new four-road locomotive shed and the expansion of the goods yard that took place following the demolition of the earlier one.

119. Bays were provided at both ends of the down platform. The one formerly used by SER trains is obscured by the coaches of the 12.7pm Eridge to Tonbridge train, as it accelerates towards the tunnel on 15th May 1964. The locomotive is Standard class 4 no. 80140. (S.C. Nash)

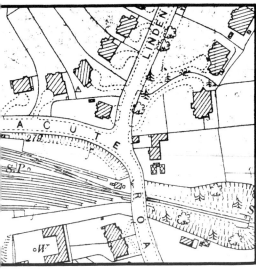

120. Twenty DEMU sets were stabled in the former goods yard and continued to be so for a while after passenger services ceased. One such unit is seen emerging from the tunnel in 1969 from the Central station and Grove Junction, subjects of a future album. (J. Scrace)

MP *Middleton Press*

Easebourne Lane, Midhurst, West Sussex, GU29 9AZ
☎ Midhurst (073 081) 3169

BRANCH LINES

BRANCH LINES TO MIDHURST	0 906520 01 0
BRANCH LINES TO HORSHAM	0 906520 02 9
BRANCH LINE TO SELSEY	0 906520 04 5
BRANCH LINES TO EAST GRINSTEAD	0 906520 07 X
BRANCII LINES TO ALTON	0 906520 11 8
BRANCH LINE TO HAYLING	0 906520 12 6
BRANCH LINE TO SOUTHWOLD	0 906520 15 0
BRANCH LINE TO TENTERDEN	0 906520 21 5
BRANCH LINES TO NEWPORT	0 906520 26 6
BRANCH LINES TO TUNBRIDGE WELLS	0 906520 32 0
BRANCH LINE TO SWANAGE	0 906520 33 9

SOUTH COAST RAILWAYS

BRIGHTON TO WORTHING	0 906520 03 7
WORTHING TO CHICHESTER	0 906520 06 1
CHICHESTER TO PORTSMOUTH	0 906520 14 2
BRIGHTON TO EASTBOURNE	0 906520 16 9
RYDE TO VENTNOR	0 906520 19 3
EASTBOURNE TO HASTINGS	0 906520 27 4
PORTSMOUTH TO SOUTHAMPTON	0 906520 31 2

SOUTHERN MAIN LINES

WOKING TO PORTSMOUTH	0 906520 25 8
HAYWARDS HEATH TO SEAFORD	0 906520 28 2
EPSOM TO HORSHAM	0 906520 30 4

STEAMING THROUGH

STEAMING THROUGH KENT	0 906520 13 4
STEAMING THROUGH EAST HANTS	0 906520 18 5
STEAMING THROUGH EAST SUSSEX	0 906520 22 3

OTHER RAILWAY BOOKS

WAR ON THE LINE The official history of the SR in World War II	0 906520 10 X
GARRAWAY FATHER AND SON The story of two careers in steam	0 906520 20 7

OTHER BOOKS

MIDHURST TOWN – THEN & NOW	0 906520 05 3
EAST GRINSTEAD – THEN & NOW	0 906520 17 7
THE GREEN ROOF OF SUSSEX A refreshing amble along the South Downs Way	0 906520 08 8
THE MILITARY DEFENCE OF WEST SUSSEX	0 906520 23 1
WEST SUSSEX WATERWAYS	0 906520 24 X
BATTLE OVER PORTSMOUTH A City at war in 1940	0 906520 29 0